Tim Ferriss: A B

Timothy Ferriss was born on July 20, 1977, in Southampton, New York. He was raised by his parents in neighboring East Hampton, NY. He has at least one brother. Little is known about his family life, but he has said that although his parents were not particularly wealthy, they always spent money on books. It is also known that he has at least one brother.

Ferriss attended St. Paul's School in Concord, New Hampshire. He spent a year in high school as an exchange student in Tokyo, Japan. It was perhaps this trip that sparked his interest in Asian studies. He also considered neuroscience, when he was planning for higher education, but quickly changed his mind once he found out he would have to kill the rats he dissected himself.

Princeton University was his first choice, because of its East Asian Studies program. However, his high school guidance counselor discouraged him from applying, ostensibly because his grades and standardized test scores were not that strong. This did not dissuade Ferriss, though—he reasoned that if he could not stand out with his grades, he could stand out in another way. He chose to focus on the admissions essay, writing about his experiences in Japan, including attending sumo practices. He was accepted and began attending in the fall of 1995. While at Princeton, he worked in a library attic before showing the entrepreneurial flair he would later make his living from. He did this by teaching seminars on how to cram for tests.

Ferriss graduated from Princeton with a Bachelor of Arts in East Asian Studies in 2000. After graduation, he moved to California, taking a job as an outside sales representative at TrueSAN Networks, a data storage company. His job was to cold-call executives at other companies and convince them to buy into a multi-million-dollar storage area network. Faced with competition from other storage area network companies like NetApp, and the industry giant EMC, Ferriss had to learn how to work smarter to make sales. As with his college application, he figured out another way around.

For example, instead of engaging in the brute force techniques of EMC, whose representatives he's written would stage practical sit-ins to make sales, he started learning the technical aspects of the product his company sold. That way, he could answer questions his prospective clients had. In addition, he would start his conversations with executives by detailing the weakest points of TrueSAN's work, believing that this would engender trust. He would also call potential clients earlier in the morning and later in the evening, when they were less likely to be screening their calls. The result was that he became not only a top salesman for TrueSAN, but also that he was outselling many of his company's competitors.

While Ferriss was still working at TrueSAN, he began his own company in 2001. It was called BrainQUICKEN and he claims he created it in less than two weeks and with $5000 in credit card debt. Formed to sell sports-focused nutritional supplements, it marketed products such as its namesake that were purported not only to improve "focus, productivity, and memory," but also "guaranteed results within 60 minutes of the first dose." Despite that claim and the other bold print on the company's website that the products were based on "[C]linically supported science used by students at Harvard, Princeton, Yale, Oxford, and by 17 world champions," this was not true. As he would later admit in his first book, the supplements were not based on real scientific data. They were cheap to make and he marketed them successfully. Although results—according to reviews—were mixed, the company was apparently successful. He was able to make a living from it once he was laid off from TrueSAN. In fact, according to Ferriss, the company was so successful that by 2004, he was earning, on average, $40,000 a month. However, that success came at a price. He had to work 14-hour days, which did not sit well with his girlfriend. In what he calls "her Dear John letter," she gave him a plaque reading, "Business hours end at 5 p.m.!"

This was a moment that Ferriss would later regard as revelatory, as he realized that making so much money meant nothing if he never had the free time to enjoy it. After a visit with a friend who had a similar lifestyle, Ferriss embarked on a one-way trip to Europe, ostensibly to relax. However, the trip at first served as shock therapy for the workaholic. Having nothing to do and not knowing how to cope with nothing to do, Ferriss panicked. He describes what he went through as a nervous breakdown, one in which he was forced to reevaluate how he worked and how he lived his life. His trip to Europe extended into one around the world. In the end, he came back to the States with a renewed focus and with plans for a book.

His new idea toward work was to streamline his responsibilities as much as possible, using ideas like delegating tasks to virtual assistants he hired on the internet and checking his email once a day. He began shaping his ideas into a book when he gave a series of lectures at his alma mater Princeton starting in

2003. Then, in 2007, he released that book, *The 4-Hour Workweek: How to Escape 9-5, Live Anywhere, and Join the New Rich*. The book was published by Crown, an imprint of Random House.

The book spent several years on *The New York Times Best Sellers List* and has been translated into 35 languages. Since its release, it has also sold over a million copies. It is the core of Ferriss's philosophy that we should be living as efficiently as possible or that life would be better spent working to live, rather than living to work. The title should not be taken literally—those titular 4 hours are the ones people should devote to the most bothersome tasks. Readers are free to devote as much time as they want to the activities they enjoy. Professional reviews of the book have been mixed, but mostly positive. The book was a particular hit in Silicon Valley, where one can understand why increased productivity would be attractive.

However, the reception was not entirely positive. Some readers have panned the book simply for being unoriginal. As many have pointed out, "work smarter, not harder" is not a revolutionary thought. In addition, many of Ferriss's ideas can be boiled down to the Pareto principle, or the 80/20 rule, which posits that 80% of many event's effects can be attributed to 20% of the causes. Still, others were troubled by what they saw as the real core of Ferriss's philosophy. While he sees it as gaming the system, many readers have seen it as cheating. After all, once he released the book and became Tim Ferriss the brand, his workweeks have certainly stretched beyond 4 hours, so one could perhaps feel justified in wariness that the author does not follow his own advice.

Other examples readers have given have been more troubling. For example, the 4-hour workweek is clearly not for everyone. Specifically, it's not for the overseas virtual assistants who earn low wages for returning Ferriss's (and other would-be 4-Hour Workweekers') emails. If everyone followed his advice, there would be no one left to outsource tasks. For people like his virtual assistants and others, including readers, who have to work, Ferriss can seem out of touch, especially when he encourages readers to quit unsatisfying jobs and then dismisses their worst-case-scenario fears.

In addition, many readers faulted Ferriss's advice on an ethical level. Many of his suggestions seem to revolve around lying or cutting corners as much as possible, which has made some readers uncomfortable. This was, after all, the book in which he revealed the truth about BrainQUICKEN, that he was really just selling hype through the company and not reliable, scientifically-tested products. In Ferriss's ideal world, apparently, no one would do the legwork to find out more. He calls this the "low information diet," or "cultivating selective ignorance," in which one avoids, for example, keeping up with current events. He has claimed in that vein that he gets his news by talking to waiters and decides which candidates get his votes by asking his friends for whom they are voting.

It is precisely this sort of corner-cutting that seems to rub some readers the wrong way and this kind of example is only the beginning. For example, Ferriss trumpets his championship gold medal from the "Chinese Kickboxing National Championships." However, even as he explains it, he won by finding loopholes. For example, he dehydrated himself before the weigh-in, getting himself down to a claimed 165 pounds, so he would be placed in a weight class with smaller men. Then he "hyperhydrated back to 193 pounds." He also found loopholes in the rules. If a combatant fell off the platform three times within a match, he was automatically disqualified and his opponent won. So Ferriss made his technique revolve around just pushing his opponents off the platform. So he may have won, but not by actually kickboxing. Indeed, one martial arts blog that printed a post from him referred to him as a "kickpusher."

In addition, although Ferriss has also named the competition he won as the United States of America Wushu-Kungfu Federation Sanshou [Chinese kickboxing] championship, there has never been any verification that this happened. The Federation's website features no mentions of Ferriss, for example, and no one has ever come forward to corroborate Ferriss's tale. That is not the case for another major achievement Ferriss likes to claim.

During his trip around the world, Ferriss ended up in Argentina. On a whim, he signed up for a beginner's tango class. He was quite taken with the dance and started studying with instructor Alicia Monti, with whom he would practice for four months. They entered the 2005 world tango dance tournament in Argentina. Ferriss says that he was the first American to enter, and that they placed in the semifinals. Unsatisfied with their results, he set his sights on a new goal: a Guinness World Record. Ferriss and Monti had completed 27 tango spins during the championship, but in September 2006, they went bigger. Appearing on *Live with Regis and Kelly*, Ferriss and Monti completed 37 tango spins, earning them the Guinness World Record.

Learning a new skill in a short period of time became a theme for Ferriss. In 2008, he shot a pilot for the History Channel called *Trial by Fire*. The premise of the series would be that Ferriss would have one week to learn a new skill. Then he would show off his skills in a final test, the "trial by fire." For example, in the pilot, he learned the art of yabusame, a Japanese practice of archery on horseback. The pilot aired, but was ultimately not picked up.

By 2010, Ferriss had become bored with BrainQUICKEN. As he told *Inc. Magazine*, "...my brain felt like a computer running antivirus software in the background. Even though the company didn't take much time to run, it was consuming more than 10 percent of my mental energy." So he sold the company in a private sale to a London-based equity firm for an undisclosed amount. By the time he sold it, it is also unclear how much income exactly he was earning from the company. As with many topics concerning Ferriss, it varies based on his telling.

That same year, Ferriss published his second book, *The 4-Hour Body: An Uncommon Guide to Rapid Fat-Loss, Incredible Sex, and Becoming Superhuman*. It was also published by Crown. Before releasing the book, Ferriss had already decided that whatever his next book's topic, it would not be about business. He noticed that many searches leading visitors to his site revolved around losing weight, so he decided to focus on physical health. In addition to the site visits, physical fitness was already a prime concern for Ferriss. He claims that he has tracked all of his workouts since he was 18. Furthermore, starting in 2004, he began keeping records of various body measurements, including his insulin levels. He believed that he had found the key to hacking one's body in the same way that he had hacked the work experience.

The book is set up almost like a choose-your-own-adventure book in that it's unnecessary to read the book straight through or even to follow all of the advice. The book is divided into segments based on topic, so that readers can dip in and choose their focus and its accompanying plan of attack. There are 50 topics covered in the book that range from all parts of a person's physical experience from diet to exercise to sleep to sex— "from the gym to the bedroom," the promotional website says. Like his previous book, *The 4-Hour Body* purports to help readers produce maximum results with minimum effort— the 80/20 principle again.

And like his previous book, many of the claims in his second book are extraordinary, seeming too good to be true. For example, in this promotional material, the reader is asked if they would like to be able to get the same or better results of sleeping for the traditional 8 hours but by sleeping only 2.

Readers are also told that they can "lose more weight than a marathoner by binging" and even reach their "genetic potential." These are obviously lofty claims, but probably par for the course for a self-help book.

These claims are based on science and experimentation, Ferriss says, and not only experimentation on himself. The promotional literature says that 200 test subjects participated in the "real-world experiments." How these test subjects were chosen and/or the details of their participation are unclear. Some reviewers have suggested that they were picked from Ferriss's Twitter followers and that their data is based on their survey responses, making any information gathered dubious and possibly biased.

Much of the book focused on diet and exercise. Ferriss did comment positively on the merits of a meat-free diet, but the bulk of the diet advice was devoted to the so-called "slow-carb diet." This is a diet that eschews dairy, white foods, simple carbohydrates, and sugar. Instead, it recommends that each meal contain a combination from five different food groups: protein, spices, healthy fats like nuts and nutritional oils, and more complex carbohydrates like legumes and vegetables. A typical meal would see its diner consuming a main portion compromising a serving of protein, legumes, and vegetables, with enough spice and healthy fats to add flavor. Healthy fats are, again, nuts and oils that are typically from single sources, such as olive oil or coconut oil. This is opposed to oils made from blends, like vegetable oil.

The participant should eat this way 6 days a week, reserving one day a week as a "cheat day," in which they can eat anything they want in the quantities they want. Cheat days are common in many diets and ways of eating, because they are believed to relieve the mental stress from dieting, which can make some dieters feel deprived. In addition, some people believe that a binge such as this keeps the body's metabolism guessing, so that metabolism does not lower as it does sometimes when people are eating a restricted diet or lower calorie load. However, not all people believe in the wisdom of cheat meals or diets. For example, for people whose weight issues have been fueled by psychological causes—like people who binge eat as a self-soothing mechanism—cheat days can be disastrous for their weight loss efforts. One cheat day can easily spill into another. Overall, none of the claims of the slow carb diet have been evaluated by an independent medical or scientific body or journal.

As with his previous book, reviews were mixed, which is understandable for a book making the kind of claims this book does. The slow carb diet and the overall eating advice were criticized, often by authors and experts who have their own diets to promote. For example, Barry Sears, who created the Zone diet, said, "Skip the 4-hour body and opt for a 24-hour-365-day-a-year body, because you need a plan that makes sense that you can live with." However, not all criticism of the eating plan was from would-be competitors. Scott Kahan of the George Washington University Weight Management Program was asked by *US News & World Reports* to evaluate the diet claims. He told them that it "sounds like another cockamamie fad diet." He was speaking specifically of the order to jettison carbs, because while cutting out or lowering carb consumption can lead to fast weight loss, many dieters find it hard to sustain a low or no carb diet. In addition, while he acknowledged the merits of a "cheat" every once in a while, he was adamant that binging was the wrong solution. He also dismissed the supplements Ferriss recommends, like garlic extract, as they are not based on any rigorous scientific review.

The magazine also asked experts about another claim in the book: the claim that people can live as healthy on 2 hours of sleep as people who get 8 hours. Ferriss's approach is part of a technique called polyphasic sleep, which, as its name indicates, involves multiple phases of sleep. In other words, those 2 hours aren't slept straight through. Instead, people who engage in polyphasic sleep take multiple naps during the day and night. More specifically, people should take 6 20-minute naps during the day and night. Ferriss does not practice polyphasic sleep regularly, confessing in the book that it's a technique he uses only for unusual situations. For example, he sleeps in a polyphasic pattern when he has to meet a deadline.

    Ferriss had his own expert on polyphasic sleep to consult for the book. Dustin Curtis, billed for the book as a polyphasic sleep expert, is actually a man of many hats, most of which revolve around web development and design. Believing that "all you really need to survive and feel rested is the REM phase," Curtis experimented with different sleep patterns until he settled on polyphasic sleep. Supposedly, polyphasic sleeping can trigger one's brain into entering REM sleep. Curtis believes that we experience only about 2 hours of REM sleep, so the 6 20-minute naps are designed to provide us with all the REM sleep that we need. There are different variations—for example, one can start with a 20-minute nap during the day and a longer chunk of sleep (about 6 hours) during the night—so people do not have to start with the intermittent naps. This may be the only form of polyphasic sleeping some people can do, since not everyone has a schedule flexible enough to allow for multiple naps during the day.

So, *US News & World Reports* investigated this claim, asking Massachusetts General Hospital's Matt Bianchi, a sleep physician and neurologist, if it were possible to function normally on only 2 hours of sleep within a 24-hour period. Bianchi replied, "The short answer is, if I may speak in medical terms, hell no." Bianchi went on to elaborate that there is no scientific data supporting the idea that sleep other than REM sleep is nonessential, making the very idea "foundationless." He also told the magazine that depriving one's self of sleep could lead to serious health issues, including ones that affect major organs, like the brain or the heart.

The final claim the magazine investigated was the only one with any scientific backing. That was the idea that one can get defined abdominal muscles with minimal exercise. While the "8 Minute Abs" video was an exercise fad in the 1990s, Ferriss is promising something even better: 6-minute abs. Professor Gary Hunter from the University of Alabama at Birmingham told the magazine that Ferriss's claims were technically true. One can get defined abdominal muscles with simple exercises. However, Hunter pointed out that definition does not mean anything if there is a layer of fat covering the abdominal muscles. Removing that layer of fat, whether through aerobic exercise or a smart diet or both, will take longer than 6 minutes.

Despite the dubious claims, the book debuted at #1 on The New York Times Best Seller List. Building on the success he had with his physiology book, he continued the theme with his next book, *The 4-Hour Chef: The Simple Path to Cooking Like a Pro, Learning Anything, and Living the Good Life*, released in 2012. As the title indicates, it is intended to be more than a mere cookbook. Ferriss pairs one of his pet topics, the idea of learning new skills in limited time, with lessons in cooking. To begin, Ferriss discusses meta-learning, the techniques by which people can learn skills faster. There are four main facets to meta-learning, Ferriss tells us. The first two are Deconstruction, in which we break a skill down to the minimum steps we need to know, and Selecting, in which we find the 20% we can learn to get us that valuable 80% result. The next two are Sequencing, in which we figure out the order in which we should learn the steps, and Stakes, where we set consequences to ensure we follow the program. The remaining five sections of the book are devoted to covering multiple parts of the cooking experience, from teaching basic cooking techniques to breaking down the science behind cooking.

Unlike his previous books, this book was not published by Crown. Instead it was published by New Harvest, a joint imprint of Houghton Mifflin Harcourt and Amazon. When it was released, it hit several bestseller charts. However, it was boycotted by some brick-and-mortar bookstores, including Barnes & Noble, because of its association with Amazon. Ferriss, always the innovator, neatly side-stepped the boycott by marketing and selling his book through non-traditional partners, including Panera Bread. He also partnered with BitTorrent, releasing a special edition with content exclusive to the torrent client.

Reviews of the book were mostly positive, with amateur reviewers generally rating it higher than his previous books. However, some professional reviewers criticized the book for its oddly limited subject matter when it came to actual dishes. It's unsurprising that the book would follow Ferriss's own way of eating, but it struck some reviewers as odd that a book that professes to teach readers to cook "like a pro" would feature no instruction for even a basic pasta. Readers do learn, however, how to gut and cook a squirrel.

While reinventing himself as a self-help guru with his popular blog, Ferriss's close interactions with Silicon Valley led to his becoming an angel investor in many startups. These include such companies as StumbleUpon, Evernote, Shopify, and TaskRabbit. The latter was a partner in releasing his third book. He has also been an advisor to startups like Uber. Ferriss has been a prolific angel investor, raising $250,000 in under an hour, for example, in 2013 for Shyp, a shipping company. However, he announced in 2015 that he was taking a break from angel investing, because he did not feel as if his contributions were having an effect and because it was too stressful.

That same year he raised money for Shyp, and in 2013, he launched Tim Ferriss Publishing, a company that releases audiobooks. Their first book release was Rolf Potts's *Vagabonding*. A month later, in December 2013, his TV series, *The Tim Ferriss Experiment*, debuted on Headline News. The series, like *Trial by Fire*, focused on Ferris learning new skills in "record time." He embarked on quests to learn new physical skills like surfing and parkour and even mental skills, like learning new languages. 13 episodes were shot for the series, but only a limited number were actually shown on television. All episodes were available through services like iTunes, though.

The following year, in 2014, Ferriss branched out to another form of media, starting the podcast, The Tim Ferriss Show. The podcast has been perhaps the most successful of all of Ferriss's ventures, or at least, the most successful whose reach we can measure. By 2016, the show's episodes had been downloaded over 70 million times. Ferriss claims it is the first business podcast to surpass 100 million downloads. Unlike his other work, which tends toward an almost manic preoccupation with hacking one's world, Ferriss's podcast features his trademark life hacking mixed in with long-form interviews with notable people. These include not only celebrities that many, if not most people would recognize, but lesser-known names like chess grand champions.

Ferriss did an interview with his friend Ryan Holliday for Observer in an article that referred to him as the "Oprah of audio" because of his massive podcast reach. In the article, one can clearly see the thought Ferriss has put into podcasting and the marketing thereof. He describes some of the techniques he's used to pull in more listeners. These include writing blog posts that are related to content discussed on the podcast and including, on his website's section for the podcast, extensive show notes with references used on the podcast. In addition, he makes listening to the show easy, producing an abbreviated version of some of the segments for people who are not ready to commit to an hour-long episode. Although he says that he recognizes the benefits of having content go viral, when it comes to listeners, he would prefer quality over quantity as long as it's steady. As he put it, "Would you rather have 100,000 people in the US, selected at random, consume your content once and know your name, or the entire audience at TED and Davos listen to your podcast at least once a month?"

The podcast, like Ferriss's blog, has been a good example of the "Tim Ferriss Effect." This refers to Ferriss's role as an influencer, and what effect appearing in his blog or on his podcast can have on a person's career or company's product. The Tim Ferriss Effect has caused sales to surge for everything from guests' books to Wild Planet brand sardines. He claims that after he mentioned the sardines on his podcast, they "sold out…in Whole Foods around the country." Like other Ferriss claims, this could not be independently verified, but other people have given testimonials to the Tim Ferriss Effect. These include author Michael Ellsberg, who coined the phrase, after a mention in a Ferriss blog post saw sales of Ellsberg's book rise. Appearing on Ferriss's blog had a better effect on sales of the book, in fact, than did appearances in more traditional media, like a write-up in *The New York Times* or a segment on CNN.

In addition to his work, Ferriss has tried to give back and not just in angel investing. While he has given money (at least six figures) to universities to be used in the research of hallucinogens to treat mental illnesses, the bulk of his philanthropic work has been focused on matters related to education. In 2014, for example, BUILD Boston, which "uses entrepreneurship to ignite the potential of youth from under-resourced communities and propel them to high school, college & career success," honored Ferriss with the BUILDer Award for Innovation and Entrepreneurship. Ferriss has especially focused on the nonprofit DonorsChoose, in which donors can fund classroom supply requests of their choice. He is a member of the nonprofit's national advisory council, and in March 2016, he and Stephen Colbert fully funded 145 projects in a "flash funding."

That same year, Ferriss released his fourth book, *Tools of Titans: The Tactics, Routines, and Habits of Billionaires, Icons, and World-Class Performers*, through Houghton Mifflin Harcourt. It featured a foreword written by Arnold Schwarzenegger, who had been a guest on the podcast. In fact, the entire book is podcast-based, drawing on the wisdom Ferris has learned from interviewing those "billionaires, icons, and world-class performers" who have appeared on his show. The book debuted at #1 on *The New York Times Best Seller List*, making it the first book based on a podcast to debut on the list.

In 2017, several of Ferriss's closest friends died within a relatively short period of time. He describes 2017 as "a very hard year, as it was for many people." That inspired him to write his fifth book, *Tribe of Mentors: Short Life*

Advice from the Best in the World. Released in November 2017, this book is somewhat of a combination of his previous book and the books before it, in that it's filled with life advice, but written in the choose-your-own-adventure style of his 4-Hour books. Overall, the book has gotten a positive reception, although some readers felt the advice was rather limited. Ferriss asked each "mentor" the same 11 questions, which obviously does not allow for much elaboration or any follow-up. In addition, some readers found the format boring, as they felt it was tedious reading the same questions over and over again.

Earlier in 2017, Ferriss began his third attempt at a television show. Called *Fear(Less) with Tim Ferriss* [sometimes stylized as *Fear{Less} with Tim Ferriss*], the show debuted in May 2017 on the AT&T Audience Network, a channel exclusive to customers of AT&T U-verse and AT&T's partner, DirecTV. Its format is more similar to his most recent books, as well as the podcast. *Fear(Less)* features interviews with "world-class performers, focusing on how they've overcome fears, made hard decisions, and won at the highest levels imaginable." The show is filmed in front of a live audience and has featured guests like magician David Blaine and comedian Bill Burr.

Also in 2017, Ferriss moved to Austin, Texas, after living in Silicon

Valley for 17 years. In an "Ask Me Anything" post on Reddit, he listed his reasons. These included that since he was no longer angel investing, he had no professional reason to remain in California. In addition, he had wanted to move to Austin for a long time, feeling a "pull" to the city. Other reasons he listed including what he described as a "mono-conversation," where all conversations revolved around technology, and the need to change one's surroundings to provoke life change. He continues to write, as well as produce his podcast.

Printed in Great Britain
by Amazon